CELEBRATING THE FAMILY NAME OF THOMPSON

Celebrating the Family Name of Thompson

Walter the Educator

Silent King Books
a WhichHead Entertainment Imprint

Copyright © 2024 by Walter the Educator

All rights reserved. No part of this book may be reproduced in any manner whatsoever without written permission except in the case of brief quotations embodied in critical articles and reviews.

First Printing, 2024

Disclaimer

This book is a literary work; the story is not about specific persons, locations, situations, and/or circumstances unless mentioned in a historical context. Any resemblance to real persons, locations, situations, and/or circumstances is coincidental. This book is for entertainment and informational purposes only. The author and publisher offer this information without warranties expressed or implied. No matter the grounds, neither the author nor the publisher will be accountable for any losses, injuries, or other damages caused by the reader's use of this book. The use of this book acknowledges an understanding and acceptance of this disclaimer.

Celebrating the Family Name of Thompson is a memory book that belongs to the Celebrating Family Name Book Series by Walter the Educator. Collect them all and more books at WaltertheEducator.com

USE THE EXTRA SPACE TO DOCUMENT YOUR FAMILY MEMORIES THROUGHOUT THE YEARS

THOMPSON

In valleys green where rivers flow,

Celebrating the Family Name of

Thompson

Beneath the skies where soft winds blow,

There stands a name of ancient might,

A beacon strong, a guiding light.

Through times of joy and trials gray,

The name of Thompson leads the way.

In days of old when knights held swords,

And kings would speak their mighty words,

The Thompsons forged their path with pride,

A lineage true, undenied.

From rolling hills to ocean's crest,

Their courage stood the hardest test.

They tilled the soil and sailed the seas,

With hands that knew both work and ease,

Their hearts were filled with honest fire,

Their spirits bold, their minds entire.

Celebrating the Family Name of

Thompson

Through winter's chill and summer's blaze,

The Thompson name endured the days.

In every storm, they stood their ground,

Their voices strong, their laughter sound,

With love that spanned from shore to shore,

A bond that time could not ignore.

Through generations, hand in hand,

They walked together, man to man.

The Thompson name, a banner high,

A star that never leaves the sky,

Through trials deep and joys so wide,

They've journeyed with their strength inside.

From father's tales to mother's song,

The Thompsons knew where they belong.

With every dawn and setting sun,

Celebrating the Family Name of

Thompson

Their legacy had just begun,

For in their blood ran stories old,

Of battles fought and fortunes bold.

Yet in their hearts, they held the truth,

That life is more than gain or youth.

In every house where they would dwell,

The Thompsons cast a gentle spell,

With kindness born from years of grace,

Celebrating the Family Name of

Thompson

And wisdom time could not erase.

ABOUT THE CREATOR

Walter the Educator is one of the pseudonyms for Walter Anderson. Formally educated in Chemistry, Business, and Education, he is an educator, an author, a diverse entrepreneur, and he is the son of a disabled war veteran. "Walter the Educator" shares his time between educating and creating. He holds interests and owns several creative projects that entertain, enlighten, enhance, and educate, hoping to inspire and motivate you. Follow, find new works, and stay up to date with Walter the Educator™

at WaltertheEducator.com

www.ingramcontent.com/pod-product-compliance
Lightning Source LLC
LaVergne TN
LVHW052009060526
838201LV00059B/3925